Communication in Marriage

21 Ways to Remarkable Communication in Marriage Without Fighting with Your Spouse

Maria Hall

Table of Contents

The author of this book has taken careful measures to share vital information about the subject. May its readers acquire the right knowledge, wisdom, inspiration, and succeed.

Introduction

Communication in marriage is one of the key pillars in a successful marriage. It is a foundation in any relationship. Just as how buildings and establishments with poor foundation may easily collapse, relationships with poor foundation – communication – may also tend to fall apart easily. If you work on improving your communication with your spouse, then you can look forward to a truly healthy, wonderful, and rewarding marriage. Communication is important because as humans, this is how we connect with one another. In marriage, you should be able to open up and talk to your spouse about anything and everything. Just imagine how wonderful it is to have someone to dream with, to discuss your fantasies and fears, to talk about your plans, and all the wonderful things this life has to offer. Of course, this wonderful "someone" ideally should be your spouse. The good news is that communication is something that you can improve and develop. It may take some time and practice, but it is worth every effort.

The beauty of having effective communication with your spouse is not just being able to talk more effectively with each other. Effective communication also opens up many doors of the heart that can spice up a relationship and finally be able to bring the fire back in your marriage. It is about being more connected to each other and having a stronger and meaningful bond. As long as you know what to do, then you can make your marriage work in a way that is full of wonder and love. This book is for the people who want to communicate more effectively and intimately with their spouse; it is for the people who want a better marriage, a marriage that is full of love, joy, and peace; this book is for the people who are willing to spend time and effort to learn and improve their relationship with their spouse. This book is for people who want their marriage to last and evolve into a beautiful partnership. If you love your spouse, then this book is definitely for you.

The importance of communication in marriage is not a secret. Unfortunately, despite so many people who wish to improve their marriage by learning how to communicate effectively, they are not able to achieve the results they desire. So, they end up facing the same problems every day with similar results still hoping that they would soon be able to improve their communication with their spouse. However, the truth is that having effective communication in marriage means more than wishful thinking. You need to know how to do it, and you should take positive actions to make it work.

This book teaches 21 effective techniques that can improve your communication in marriage without having to resort to fighting or other meaningless arguments. Carefully study these techniques and apply them in your life. Positive changes may take time to happen, but they are possible and are well within your reach. This book gives you the key to a happier marriage. It is now up to you to take action and make some positive changes in your marriage.

There are plenty of books on this subject on the market, thanks for choosing this one! Every effort was made to ensure it is consist of as much useful information as possible. Please enjoy!

1: Active Listening

When it comes to communication, it is a common advice that you should listen to the other person. However, there are many people who are still not able to follow this. Even those who are already aware of this basic rule in communication also fail to observe this practice.

So, how do you really listen?

Unfortunately, many people think that hearing what the other person is saying is the same as listening. It is worth noting that hearing is just a part of listening. Listening creates a deeper connection between you and the person whom you are talking with. If you want to be a good and effective communicator, then you should learn active listening.

Active listening is not just a way to listen to another person. Rather, it also assures the other person that you are truly listening to them. This is important as it will make the other person feel loved and that you are giving him or her your time and your attention. A good example of how this works is by repeating what your spouse is saying. You should also ask follow-up questions. For example, if your spouse says something about her day, ask her more about it. For example, if she just tells you that her day was fine, ask her what happened. The key to active listening is to continue the flow of communication and to maintain your interest in what your spouse is saying. Here is an example of what active listening is:

Spouse: It was a tiring day today.

You: Oh, is everything alright? What happened?

Spouse: I had to do extra work because my colleague was absent.

You: Oh, it must be tiring to do extra tasks than you normally do. Must have been challenging!

~ ~ ~

In this scene, you could have just ended the conversation when your spouse told you how he or she feels. But, you ask questions to keep the conversation going and to show your interest in what he or she says and feels. You can even repeat and confirm the exact words your spouse has said. This simple act of validating and confirming your spouses' words and feelings is very powerful. You do need to judge, understand or make sense of what your spouse is saying. Just listen to their words and validate them. It makes the other person feel that he or she is understood and this builds trust and comfort.

Active listening is an act of love. When you actively listen to another, you give him or her the time and opportunity to express himself. As he opens himself up to you, you assure him that you are there for him and that you are listening to him. Of course, the same applies if you are the man in the relationship. Active listening is something that both parties should do for the communication to be more effective. After all, true communication is a two-way process whereby the parties take turns between talking and listening.

Active listening is a key to a healthy communication, especially if both spouses mutually observe it. If you are not yet used to doing active listening, then it is never too late for you to start learning it. It is much easier than you might think, and it will make your spouse feel more special and loved.

Active listening is something that you can do every time that you engage in a conversation. Now, some people have the habit of only listening attentively if the topic interests them, but fail to give the same attention when talking about something that only interests their spouse. Keep in mind that you should always try to listen attentively to what your spouse tells you. Even if you do not find the subject of the conversation to be interesting or important enough, exercise the patience to listen. If you cannot be interested in the topic, at least be interested in your spouse.

So, the next time that you talk with your spouse, remember to stop whatever it is that you are doing and actively listen to him or her. Repeat certain statements to show that you can follow the conversation, and also use follow-up questions. Another key to active listening is to help your spouse to express himself or herself. This is why some people say that it is "easy" to talk with a certain person.

If a person knows how to do active listening, then the person with whom he or she is talking with will most likely feel good, more open and relaxed. This is a very important skill to learn when it comes to building effective communication.

2: Share

Effective communication is a two-way process. It is not just about listening to your spouse. You will also get the chance to talk and share something with your spouse. You can share much more than you think. In fact, the more personal it is, the better. But, you do not always have to say something deep and meaningful. You can simply talk about your day at work or what you think about the movie that you just watched. The important thing is to share something and connect with your spouse. It is also advised that you exercise some humor. Laughing with your partner is good. Laughter is often a sign that you are enjoying each other's company. Learn to laugh together and be happy.

Although you can share anything, even the smallest and most trivial of things, do not be content with just sharing about your day at work. It is strongly advised that you also share your feelings. Talk to your spouse about your relationship. It is also a good practice to talk about your future plans together and see if you are in the right direction to achieve your dreams.

As the saying goes: "Sharing is caring." It is also an act of trust where you share a part of yourself with another person. Most of the time, those who are keeping so many secrets from their spouse are the ones who experience serious relationship problems. The more open you are to each other, the healthier your relationship will be.

Avoid the trap of being too narcissistic. Some people only care about what they share and fail to recognize how the other person responds. Worse, they do not even want to listen to what the other person wants to say. They just care about their own story. Sharing is also a communication, which means that it is a two-way process. You talk, but you also have to listen to what your spouse has to say. Do not make the conversation be only about yourself. Learn to take turns and give your spouse a chance to open up and share something as well.

Would it not be great when you can share anything and everything with each other? Well, the good news is that this is exactly the kind of bond marriage is all about. Unfortunately, many people these days are used to keeping secrets from their spouse. Sometimes they put so many walls in their married life that their friends know them more than their spouse does. If there are similar issues in your marriage, then it is time for you to make some positive changes. As according to the poet, Rumi, "Your task is not to seek for love, but merely to seek and find all the barriers within yourself that you have built against it." Before there can be a channel where you and your spouse can share everything freely with each other, you must first take down your walls, and be ready to share who you are with your spouse. Needless to say, you should also encourage your spouse to do the same. You can do this simply by asking your spouse to share something with you, by asking questions, or simply by encouraging him or her to share something with you. There is really no right or wrong way of doing this. But, of course, before you can expect your spouse to share something with you, you must first earn his or her trust. Trust is something that is built over time. The fact that you are married shows that you trust each other. However, if this is not the case, then make yourself worthy of being trusted, and you can do this by trying to always be true to your spouse.

Try to share your innermost feelings with your spouse. It is always a pleasure to hear confessions of love and longing from someone who is special to you. Feel free to share your day with your spouse, but also make it a point to share with your spouse how you feel about him or her and your relationship. Of course, this may not always be something that is positive in nature. After all, you should also deal with problems from time to time, which is normal in marriage. However, as much as possible, keep your focus and topic of conversations on something that is positive and would improve your relationship. A good example of this is sharing your plans for each other for the future, such as how you see yourselves in 10 years from now, and so on. It is always good to have a plan and be sure to intimate your spouse about your plans in life. Since you are married, you are no longer alone in this journey of life. Every step that you make, you do so with your spouse beside you. This is a way to convey how important and meaningful he or she is to you.

A married life is actually a life of sharing. It is the kind of relationship where you can share everything with another person. Of course, this other person would also share everything with you. It is a life that is supposed to be full of love. Therefore, do not let the outside world change the value of your relationship with each other. Do your best to your relationship and give everything to your spouse. The true meaning of sharing is not just about sharing stories and things but is more about giving your whole self to your lover. Indeed, sharing is an act of divine love.

3: Constructive Criticism

In a relationship, you cannot always expect to agree with your partner. It is not always easy to give and receive a criticism; however, sometimes, this can be important. To maintain the positive nature of a conversation, you should learn to give constructive criticism. It is constructive in the sense that it is helpful and does not judge a person. Instead of judging or dictating, a constructive criticism offers suggestions. Also, instead of focusing on the person, it focuses on the situation. For example, if your spouse has a particular habit that you do not like, make it clear that what you do not like is the habit and not him or her as a person. Do not say, "I do not like you." Instead, say, "I do not like it when you..." By doing so, you are not blaming the person directly. This is important to learn as you would definitely have to give some constructive criticisms from time to time. Another benefit of constructive criticism is that it tends to improve a person. Of course, it is also important that you should be mature enough to take constructive criticism. Instead of feeling bad about it, you should appreciate that your partner has taken the courage and opportunity to give you constructive criticism. It is not always easy to do so. It only means that your spouse really cares about you.

If you are the one who is going to give constructive criticism, then you need to be careful about it. Keep in mind that every constructive criticism that you make can hurt your spouse. Avoid using harsh words and phrases. Make it as gentle as possible, but be sure to deliver your message clearly. Also, do not expect to control your partner by giving him constructive criticisms every now and then. Keep in mind that a constructive criticism is only a suggestion and is not meant to dictate to your spouse how he should think or what he should do.

It is good for a couple to get used to giving and receiving constructive criticisms from each other. Do not be too sensitive when you receive one. Once you realize that your spouse is not your enemy but someone who truly loves you, then you would understand that any constructive criticism that you get from him or her is not meant to discourage or embarrass you.

But, what if after receiving constructive criticism, you still get really hurt? After all, not everything can be worded gently. In this case, you should not hesitate to talk with your spouse about it. In marriage, it is important that you are open to each other. You should be able to voice out your feelings and thoughts without any worry. It is also a kind of teamwork. So, if your spouse tells you that she is hurt because of what you just said, do not ignore him or her and move on to a different topic as others do. Instead, you should talk to your spouse more about it. Explain in a gentle way why you said something like that. Be sure that you have a good reason for it, and let him or her know that you said it for their own good. And, of course, always reassure your love for him or her.

The truth is that nobody enjoys receiving any kind of criticism, even if it is constructive criticism. So, be very careful with your choice of words. The key is to focus on the positive side. For example, instead of saying, "You left the light on last night." you can just say, "Honey, please don't forget to turn off the light." If you want, you can even add a kiss on the lips. This is the way to change something positively. You do not really have to make a direct critic of something. Also, take note that when you give constructive criticism to your spouse, you should do so as an act of love and not a way of simply making him or her feel bad.

One effective technique to give a criticism in a positive and loving way is the *sandwich technique* where the bread represents praise, and the peanut butter represents the corrective feedback or criticism. To do this, praise your spouse first for the things you appreciate about him/her or about the things he/she did recently, then give your brief and honest criticism, and end it by saying a positive note about them. Take note, though, to try to make the genuine compliments short. Otherwise, it can bury or discount the criticism you want to point out. Also, make your criticism short, but still clear and thorough. Three or more criticisms may be too much for your spouse to handle.

As much as possible, avoid giving constructive criticisms. But, of course, there will surely be moments when doing so would be unavoidable. Just keep it as light but clear as possible. You can also say or do something nice to your spouse after giving constructive criticism to counterbalance its effects. Still, as a couple, you should be mature enough to handle and talk about constructive criticisms. It is part of life, including married life. Also, do not forget that the intention behind every constructive criticism is always good, so do not be too sensitive. Learn to recognize it as an act of love.

4: Be Polite

Whether you are giving a constructive criticism or simply talking with your spouse, it is always a good idea to be polite. When engaged in a conversation, being polite can be expressed by being careful with your choice of words, as well as your manner of talking. Be gentle with your speech. If you think that you may have issues with being polite, a good practice is to make it a habit of thinking of a better way of saying what is on your mind. Remember that the words you choose are important as the words are the ones that convey your meaning. Of course, how you convey those words, such as your manner and tone of speech also matters.

It is easy to be polite when things are going smooth and easy. However, as a couple, you can expect to encounter some rough roads along the way. Other than being polite, you also need to be patient. The reason is that when you run out of patience, then it would be hard to remain polite. As they say, "Patience is a virtue." This is true in marriage. From time to time, you will have to be patient with your spouse. If you lose patience, then you will also not be able to control yourself. When this happens, it will be difficult for you to remain polite.

Take note that being polite does not mean that you should not be yourself. Well, unless you consider yourself as a rude person, then perhaps this is the chance for you to make some positive changes in your life.

You should understand that being polite does not mean that you are still shy with each other. Just because you get to learn to be yourself with each other does not mean that being polite is no longer important. You should still be sensitive to how your spouse may feel when you do or say something.

Being polite can be as simple as adding "please" when you ask for something. Also, do not forget to say, "Thank you." when your spouse does something for you. By being polite, you create a positive atmosphere that is conducive to positive energies like love, compassion, understanding, and kindness.

But, of course, you are only human. You cannot be expected to be polite all the time. However, try to be polite as much as possible. If you feel like your patience is about to run out, then that is the time to call for a timeout. It is better not to talk with your spouse for few hours than to spend that much time yelling at each other. Hence, if you think that you cannot handle a good conversation at the moment, then learn to step back for a while and just come back when you are ready.

If you ever fail to be polite and totally mess up, do not hesitate to ask for forgiveness. After all, being polite all the time is not an easy thing to do. Being polite is also an effective way to avoid getting into an argument. It gives a message that you are not talking to argue but that you want to resolve the issue peacefully. It is also a good protective measure to keep the conversation calm and under control. Being polite is just like improving a certain behavior or attitude. The more times that you work on it, the easier it will be for you to be polite. Soon enough, it will just come naturally to you to talk gently and use good manners.

5: Be Understanding

Understanding each other is an important element of communication. In fact, every time a person talks, he or she expects to be understood. Understanding your partner may be easy; however, there may be times when being understanding can be a challenge. The key to being understanding is to learn how to listen attentively. By listening and keeping an open mind, you will be able to understand better what your spouse is telling you. Understanding is not about accepting whatever your spouse is telling you. Rather, it is more about being able to view the situation from your partner's point of view. By seeing the subject from the point of view of your spouse, you will have a better understanding of whatever it may be that your partner is trying to communicate with you.

Being understanding is not just about being logical. In fact, some decisions in life are not really based on reason but on strong emotions. Hence, when you understand your partner, you should also try to understand him or her on an emotional level. This is true especially for women since women tend to be more emotional than men when making decisions. Therefore, if you are the man, make an effort to understand how your wife feels.

A common mistake is pretending that you understand something instead of admitting that you cannot understand what your partner is telling you. If you just pretend to know it, then you will most probably fail to make an appropriate response. Instead of faking it, you should ask your partner more questions to make it clearer. Once you can truly understand your partner, then it will be easier for you to comfort him or her.

Although understanding is important, there may come a time in a relationship where you will not be able to understand your spouse completely no matter what he or she tells you. This is true, especially if it is something that he is passionate about and of which you do not know much about. For example, if your spouse has a passion for writing poems but which happens to be not in your area of interest, you can still listen to your spouse. Although people want to be completely understood when they talk, sometimes what they really want is simply someone who can listen to them. After all, it is not uncommon for people not to understand themselves. Sometimes what people want is simply to have someone who would listen to them and who would not judge them no matter what they say or do.

To be understood, you also need to understand. Sometimes trying to see things from your spouse's perspective can help. In a communication, both parties must exert effort to understand each other. If only one person is willing to understand, then that is not effective communication. Communication should be mutual. If you want to talk, you should also give a turn for the other person to talk. If you want to be understood, then you should also understand your spouse. Effective communication is a two-way and mutual process; it is not one-sided.

Many couples find understanding to be a bit of a challenge. Do not be discouraged if you're having a hard time understanding your spouse. The failure to understand your spouse roots back to how you listen to him or her. Active listening and understanding come hand in hand. By being an effective listener, you become more understanding. On the contrary, if you fail to listen sincerely to what your partner is saying, then you will have a hard time understanding him or her. The *timer technique* can help you (and your spouse) to become a more active listener. In this technique, you and your spouse should promise each other to listen with full, undivided attention without interruption. For example, each one gets 10 minutes to speak their mind and then take turns. Each of you gets 10 minutes to speak out your thoughts and 10 minutes to listen very carefully to each other. Try to be non-judgmental during these 10 minutes. You do not need to analyze or make sense of what your spouse is saying. Just be present and listen attentively and try to understand the situation from their point of view.

6: Stay Calm

You should aim to stay calm when you communicate with your spouse. Do not let negative emotions like anger, disappointment, or even stress, to get in the way. When you are calm, you get to think more clearly, and you can also understand each other more easily.

It is easy to stay calm when you are having a fun time with your spouse. But, how do you stay calm when you are under pressure? For example, how do you stay calm when you are facing financial problems? You need to understand that calmness is in the mind. If you can control your mind, you can remain calm as much as you like despite the circumstances of a situation. The key is to view the problem or whatever it is that is making you uncomfortable as something that is outside of yourself — and this, in fact, is true. By doing so, you get to think outside the box and see the problem from a new and clear perspective. Now, if the problem has something to do with the attitude of your spouse or something that he has done, you should view it as something separate from him. This is why when you talk about it, you do not blame your spouse directly.

Instead, you should focus on the behavior or action that you do not like.

You should also avoid raising your voice. Never shout at your spouse. Shouting often destroys the calm and peace in a relationship. If it is your partner who shouts at you, do not respond by yelling back at him or her. Never answer anger with anger. In a marriage, you should learn to adjust. If you notice that your partner is having a difficult time and is unable to control his or her temper, then you can express your love by comforting him or her and avoiding all sorts of arguments. Always aim to be polite and gentle when you talk.

Unfortunately, you may not always be able to control yourself all the time. There are times when you might be completely out of the mood to exercise any patience. When this happens, and you notice that your spouse is about to create an argument, you should tell him that you are not yet ready to talk. However, assure him that you will soon talk with him about it, but that first, you need to give time for yourself. Again, it is worth remembering that you should avoid getting attached to a problem or any other external thing. If there is any attachment that is encouraged, then that is only for you to be more attached to your spouse, and nothing else. Cool down as much as you can. If you want, you can listen to some relaxing music or even treat yourself an ice cream. Once you feel relaxed and ready to talk, you can now approach your spouse and talk to him or her about the problem.

Meditating and mindfulness can help you to be calm – not just for certain moments, but for the long-term as well. Take time to practice your breathing in a quiet, peaceful place. It could be in your garden or somewhere that has no distractions. To meditate, sit or lie comfortably. Then, close your eyes. While your eyes are closed, practice your breathing. Do not try to control it. Just breathe naturally. Focus only on your breathing. If your mind starts to wander, simply put your attention back to the pace of your breathing. By meditating, you're relaxing and helping yourself to handle external stressors better. It will help you become a calmer person. Not to mention, it is also healthy for you as it is proven to be therapeutic.

If you notice that your partner is no longer calm and is raising his or her voice, be the mature one to keep quiet and lessen the tension. Answering anger with anger can seriously injure a relationship. A common mistake is getting angry at a situation but then releasing that anger at your spouse. Do not forget that your spouse is not your problem, and being angry at your spouse would not solve your problem. Instead, love your spouse, treat him well, and solve the problem together as a team.

The moment that you lose your calm is also the moment when arguments can take place. The problem here is that this often leads to more arguments. Soon enough, the couple will just find themselves hating each other. This is wrong because the truth is that your spouse is on your side, and he or she is your best ally. Remember: It is better to lose to an argument than end up losing each other. Problems come and go, but true love can stay forever.

7: Be Open

Spouses should be open to each other. When you look at your spouse, it is a reflection of yourself that you should see. This is because you belong to each other. Ideally, you should tell your spouse everything. your dreams, fears, plans in life, secrets, fantasies, and others. For this to happen, you need to be open to each other. This is also something that does not happen overnight. Rather, you should always try to practice be open to your spouse.

If you notice that your spouse is opening up to you, then be kind enough to listen attentively to him or her. This does not only improve the level of communication in marriage but also improves your relationship with each other.

An important part of being open to each other is having acceptance. You should expect that not everything that your spouse would tell you will be something that you will like. You need to accept your spouse, including his or her weaknesses. Do not worry; this is a mutual thing, which means that your spouse should also accept you, as well as your imperfections. If you truly love each other, then this would not be hard to do.

Having a relationship where you are completely open to each other is important. It is an amazing experience to know that you can just be yourself and that the other person truly accepts you and loves you for just being you, without any mask or pretense. If you think that you and your spouse are not yet that open to each other, then it is not yet too late. You can always start *now*.

If your spouse is not too open to you, you can encourage him or her to be more open by taking the first step: Be the first one to open up to him or her. You are free to share with him anything you like to. This will make him or her feel that opening up is okay and that he or she has nothing to worry about. Take note that you are not just doing this for him or her. You are doing it for yourself and mainly for each other.

Opening up does not have to be dramatic. You can do so with some humor and laughter. Of course, this will depend on the topic, but the important thing here is to be open to each other. Be as transparent as possible. By continuously exercising openness and acceptance, you can build trust. As you may already know, trust is very important in any relationship, especially in marriage. When trust is broken, love also begins to falter. In fact, being open is already an act of trust.

The common problem is that some couples start out having a fine relationship where they are completely open to each other, but then the level of their openness decreases after some time. This usually happens when the relationship starts to lose its "magic." Of course, the relationship does not really lose its magic unless you allow it. Therefore, keep in mind that you should apply all the techniques in this book. You cannot just choose one and ignore the others. Being open also means working on developing your relationship.

There are many things that you can be open about. Although you can share anything, it is strongly suggested that you focus more on being open about things that are positive in nature, such as your love for your spouse and how much he or she means to you. The key is to focus on the positive. This is also the way to having a positive relationship. Of course, from time to time, you can also be open about something that may not be that pleasant. Just do not focus too much on the negative things as they tend to weaken a relationship. Your spouse might already have problems that he is facing at work. When he talks to you, it would be nice if he gets to hear about beautiful and pleasant things. This can make a big difference in his busy world.

When being open is mutually done, and if there is acceptance, then a meaningful relationship can take place. After all, many people in the world are just looking for someone who would accept them for who they are. This acceptance means that you continue to love a person despite being fully aware of his/her imperfections and weaknesses. As you can see, being open is an important act of love. It is also by opening up that you give and receive love. Like a flower that opens its petals to receive the sun, you should open your heart to your lover.

8: Show Appreciation

Show your spouse that you appreciate him or her. If he or she does something that you like, be sure to let him know about it and give him a nice compliment. Needless to say, this also applies if you are the man in the relationship. Make sure your spouse knows how much you appreciate her and what she does. A good way to show one's appreciation is by giving a good compliment. It does not have to be too exquisite. Something as simple as saying, "You are beautiful." is a good way to let her know that you appreciate her beauty. You do not need to use elaborate words just to express your appreciation. You just have to be clear. For example, if you see your husband tired because of work, you can kiss him on the lips and tell him that you appreciate how much he works for the family.

Never let your spouse feel that he or she is being taken for granted. Instead, make him feel special and loved all the time. This is not just about communication but also about building a better and stronger relationship. Of course, an effective way of doing this is by expressing your appreciation. The more intimate your relationship is, the easier it will be for you to connect with each other.

Expressing one's appreciation for another can be as good as the one who is receiving it. Unfortunately, many people are not used to expressing appreciation. Many are shy or are simply uncomfortable with it. If you think that you are one of these people, then it is time for you to make some changes and not take your loving relationship for granted. Make it a point to show and tell your spouse how important he or she is to you and how happy you are for being able to love him or her every day. Do not hold back anything. Show your appreciation and express your emotions. Expressing your appreciation is also an excellent way to learn to be more open with each other.

Now, there are those who are good at showing appreciation but then when the same thing happens over a long period of time, the tendency is to feel less appreciative of it. This is also something that is very common. For example, if our spouse is always the one who prepares your breakfast before you go to work, perhaps in the first few weeks you would always show how touched you are. However, after about a year or two, it would be considered as something normal. Worse, it might even be felt as an obligation that she has to cook your breakfast every time you go to work. This is the danger of getting into a routine. But, it should be noted that a routine is not completely bad. The only danger is if you fail to see the meaning behind the routine. In our given example, do not just see it as receiving food from your spouse. Rather, think about her efforts in preparing it, and also consider how many times she has cooked your meals. This is more than enough reason for you to feel gratitude and be happy. Of course, all thanks to your spouse. To make her feel that you appreciate her efforts and that you are not taking her for granted, you can treat her on a date and tell her directly how happy you are that she is always cooking your breakfast. Of course, there are many other examples that you can come up with on how you can express your appreciation. The thing is that every time your spouse does something for you, be sure to recognize it — and make her aware that you do.

Many couples do not really have a problem with having an appreciation for their partner. However, the problem is not being able to show it. Do not expect for your partner just to know that you appreciate him. Make sure that he feels it, too. To do this, you need to express your appreciation through positive actions. Expressing one's appreciation also encourages the other spouse to do the same. This is one of the benefits of showing that you appreciate somebody. AS the saying goes, "Do unto others what you would have them do unto you." Hence, if you want to be appreciated, and if you want to feel that your spouse appreciates you, then do not wait for your spouse to do it for you. Instead, take the step and be the one to express to your spouse that you appreciate him. Most likely, you will end up showing appreciation for each other, which greatly improves a relationship. This, of course, has the natural effect of improving your communication with each other.

9: Avoid Arguments

Nobody really wins an argument, especially if you are arguing with your spouse. Keep in mind that you should be on the same side as your spouse, so there is no point for you to be arguing. Of course, this does not mean that you cannot discuss matters and disagree with each other from time to time; however, it is important for you to keep the conversation constructive. Unfortunately, many arguments go out of control that the couple ends up fighting even over a subject that is not even important. They end up hating each other instead of the subject that they are talking about.

Instead of arguing, you should learn to talk gently and kindly. Also, do not confuse the problem with your spouse. Feel free to hate the problem, but always love your spouse. The married life is not always a smooth path. From time to time, you will have to face problems as a couple. These problems can often tempt you to argue against each other, but do not allow this to happen. Arguing with your spouse will only make things more complicated. The truth is that there is no need for you to argue with each other. Instead, you should learn to talk with each other properly. The key is not to be attached to the problem. This way you can talk about it without a strong emotional attachment. This will also help you discuss the matters more clearly with each other. You should realize that your spouse is your ally and not your enemy.

But, what should you do if you are already in an argument? After all, you cannot always avoid an argument especially when your spouse is being too pushy to argue with you. In this case, you should learn to argue politely and reasonably. Take note that your objective here is not really to argue with your spouse, but to solve the problem so that the peace in your marriage can be restored. Once you get good at handling tough situations, you will realize that you can still talk about problems and even argue without sacrificing a peaceful atmosphere. After all, as a couple, you should already expect to face problems every now and then. Hence, it is not good to get used to arguing. Instead, get used to solving problems as a team.

It is true that nobody wins an argument, especially if you are arguing with your spouse. Just the fact that you are arguing only shows that there is already a problem in your communication. Do not worry; this is something that you can fix. Another problem with arguing is that it creates a negative environment for carrying out a conversation. If all else fails, just remember that it is better to lose an argument than to offend your spouse. The good thing is that arguments do not really last long. The pressure tends to subside after a few minutes or a few hours. So, after giving your spouse time to calm down and relax, you can now approach him and talk with him in a kind and polite manner.

10: Spend Quality Time Together

Another effective way of improving the level of communication in marriage is by spending quality time with your spouse. This is the time for you to take a break from work and your busy life, and simply enjoy the day with your spouse. You might want to ask your partner out on a date. It does not have to be too expensive. If you want, you can just have a movie night at home. The important thing here is to do something that you both enjoy together. This is a good way to strengthen the bond in marriage, as well as for increasing the level of intimacy.

Effective communication becomes easy and natural when you have a good relationship with your spouse. Spending quality time together from time to time is important in a relationship. When you do, avoid talking about problems and things that may lead to an argument. Even just for this moment, just enjoy being together and express your love for each other.

Make it a habit of spending quality time with your spouse. Going on a date, even just a simple one, should be a priority. If you can always find time for work, then all the more reason that you should make time for your spouse.

It is easier to talk to people when they are happy or in a good mood. This makes quality time one of the best opportunities to talk with your spouse about anything. If you want to improve your communication with each other, then this is your chance to do it. Spending quality time is also a way to reaffirm your love and to be more connected to each other on a deeper level. As you can see, spending quality time with your spouse is very important in marriage. Studies also show that couples who make the effort to go out on a date on a regular basis have a higher chance of making their marriage work than those who do not.

Spending quality time with your spouse is one of the best moments in your life. After all, why do you have to work so hard if not for your spouse or family? You need to realize just how blessed you are for having a spouse. Do not take your spouse for granted, and be sure to always spend time together. You do not have to do anything that is grand, but always try to enjoy life together. In fact, what people call as *little things* in life are actually the best things if you enjoy them with someone. As the saying goes, "Happiness is only real when shared."

11: Use Affirmations

You should also learn the use of affirmations. Affirmations are words and/or acts that affirm your love for each other. When was the last time that you told your spouse that you love him or her? When was the last time that you bought him a gift to show how you appreciate and love him? Marriage is like a flower that you water every day for it to bloom and grow. In the same way, you should affirm for each other regularly. It is not enough that your spouse knows that you love him. You should also make him or her feel it. Fortunately, there are more than a thousand ways to express one's love for another. Over the years that you will spend together as a couple, you will definitely not run out of ways to show your love and make your spouse feel it more deeply.

Affirming one's love is done by continuously loving your spouse. There are many ways to affirm your love, whether through your words or deeds. Never forget to tell your spouse that he or she is important to you.

Avoid saying "I love you." as a mere habit. Those are three sacred and powerful words that deserve attention and respect. Say "I love you." because you mean it, and say it as you look straight into your beloved's eyes.

Affirming one's love should not be seen as a duty or obligation. After all, if you are truly in love with your spouse, then affirming your love for him or her would be a natural expression of yourself. Also, you will never run out of ways to affirm your love. It can be as simple as cooking his favorite dishes, buying a surprise gift, among many others. It can also be a surprise dinner date at some luxurious restaurant, a special trip for a vacation, etc. There is no limit to how you can affirm your love for your spouse because love is infinite.

The use of kind words when you give compliments is one of the best ways to express love. When you do this, be sure that you also use the right tone of voice. Words alone are nothing — you also need to be sincere. If you are sincere enough, and if you express your message the right way, then your spouse would feel it.

Affirming your love to your spouse is something that you should continuously do without an end. If you truly love your spouse, then this is something that is very easy and natural to do. People who are in love usually affirm their love even without thinking about it. Unfortunately, during the long course of a marriage and because of the demands of modern life, you may have to remind yourself every now and then to do some positive action to affirm your love to your spouse. This is good, and you should turn this into a habit. Make sure to affirm your love at least once every week.

12: Use Physical Touch

Although communication is primarily about the use of words, you should not underestimate the power of using physical touch. Placing your hand on your spouse's lap or holding his hand can help you deliver a more powerful statement. Touching your partner is a quick and effective way to build a connection. It is also a suggested way to increase intimacy. A touch instantly delivers a message that you are there for him or her, and it is also comforting. When skins touch, warmth is felt, and this easily gives comfort.

Sometimes a touch can even deliver a more sincere message than talking. For example, embracing your partner after an argument is a good way of saying that you are sorry. Yes, you are not limited to just using your hands. The body can communicate with another body. It can express emotions and heighten intimacy.

Avoid becoming like other couples who take these things for granted. Sometimes they hold hands without even appreciating the meaning behind it. Make the commitment that everything that you do with your partner will be meaningful and sincere.

It is not uncommon for couples to suddenly lose this kind of physical intimacy. But although this may be considered normal, do not let this happen to you in your marriage. Do not take these things for granted. A good way to keep it meaningful is by telling your partner how much you like holding his or her hand or having his hand on your lap, or whatever physical connection that he does. This way he will be aware that you recognize his actions and that you like them. This will help to reinforce those actions and even turn them into a habit.

Do not lose the physical intimacy in your marriage. This does not refer to just sex but embraces all forms of physical connection, such as embracing each other and holding hands. Sometimes a simple touch can speak a thousand words. Its comfort can easily be felt. It is sad to say that many couples these days no longer hold each other's hands. According to a study, holding hands is a sign of a strong relationship and intimacy. It is a sign that you are with and for each other. The next time that you talk with your spouse try to add some physical touch. Do it gently and sincerely. It is like making gestures but is something that is more easily felt by the other person.

13: Make Eye Contact

As the saying goes, "The eyes are the windows to the soul." Make it a habit of making eye contact when you talk with your spouse. It ensures that you have your attention fixed on him or her, and it also makes the conversation more intimate.

It is also suggested to make eye contact when you say something that is meaningful, like how happy you are that he is your husband, etc. Eye contact will make your statement more truthful and sincere. But, of course, you need to be sure that what you are telling your spouse is also true. Making eye contact is not a trick to make your spouse believe your words. Rather, you should use it because you mean what you are saying.

Making eye contact is not hard. In fact, if you are truly sincere of what you are saying, if you mean every word, you will find that making eye contact is actually something that comes naturally. Hence, the key to making eye contact is simply to be truthful and sincere when you talk with your spouse.

Unfortunately, some people really find making eye contact to be very uncomfortable. In this case, what you can do is to look at the edge of your partner's eye instead of looking directly into his or her eyes. This way it will look as if you are staring directly at him or her even if you are only staring at a corner of his eye. Of course, it is still strongly suggested that you should get used to looking straight into your spouse's eyes instead of "faking" it. After all, when you express sincerity, then it should be real.

Unfortunately, many couples these days lose the magic of looking into each other's eyes. Some no longer look at each other's eyes even when they make love. Try looking at your spouse the way you used to in the early part of your relationship. Once again, appreciate how he or she looks. This is not really about physical beauty, but by looking into your spouse's eyes, you can remind yourself of all the love that you have shared.

14: Admit Your Mistakes

You should learn to admit your mistakes when you are wrong. Do not let your pride or ego cause you to ruin your beautiful relationship. Keep in mind that you do not always have to be right. From time to time, surely you will commit some mistakes, and that is normal. Just be sure to learn from every mistake and use it to become a better lover to your spouse. It is unfortunate that there are people who would not admit their mistakes at the expense of their relationship. As a spouse, you need to learn to lower your pride when you talk with your husband or wife.

Admitting your mistakes is not just about admitting it to yourself. You should also share them with your spouse. Do not forget to say that you are sorry and let her know what you are sorry for. If you have committed a mistake, tell her about it and then apologize. This way he or she will know that you are really aware of your mistake and that you recognize your fault. Now, if it is your spouse who is admitting her mistakes, then be kind enough to listen to her and extend forgiveness. After all, in marriage, mistakes are definitely bound to happen. The important thing is to learn from every mistake and use that knowledge to make your marriage bond stronger.

Some people find it hard to admit their mistakes. Before you admit them to your spouse, you first need to admit them to yourself. The problem is usually because of pride. Again, when you are talking with your spouse, the man/woman of your life, throw your pride away for it will not do you any good. Remember to let go of your pride and hold on to your spouse.

It is not always easy to admit one's mistakes. Sometimes it can take time. After all, the first step is for you to find it if you are really mistaken. Feel free to spend some time to ponder about the situation. Once it is clear to you that you are the one who is at fault, then admit it and ask for forgiveness from your spouse.

Some people simply admit a "mistake" even without knowing what it is. They do so for the sake of saving the relationship without any argument. This is wrong because it does not make you understand the problem. Hence, there is a chance that you will fall into the same problem again in the future. Also, do not forget that sincerity is important in marriage. If you admit a mistake even when you do not know what it is, that is not considered sincere. If you find it confusing, do not hesitate to ask questions to your spouse. Let him know that you want to understand what you have done that made him upset so that you will not do it again. Of course, the same applies if you are the man in the relationship.

It is okay to admit your mistakes, especially to your spouse. Admitting one's mistakes is also a sign of humility and sincerity. It also shows that you lower your pride for the sake of your relationship. It shows that you are willing to learn and improve yourself to be a better spouse. So, when you make mistakes, admit them, learn from them, and then do everything that you can to be a better spouse.

15: Be Kind

Be kind to your partner. Always. No matter how problematic and busy life can be, do not forget the fact that your spouse is one of the most important person in the world for you. Due to some circumstances, people can sometimes be in a bad mood that they can be hard to deal with. Be kind, anyway. After all, arguing with your spouse will never do your relationship any good. Unfortunately, some people take their spouse for granted just after a few years in a relationship. If you can be kind to your boss no matter how irritating and insulting he or she can be, then with all the more reason that you should be kind to your spouse.

Be kind not only in your thoughts, but you should also express it through your actions. It also means being a gentleman (if you are the male). Hence, remind yourself to open the car door for her, avoid getting upset and learn to control your temper, and all other things that you would do to express love and kindness.

Being kind may also mean treating your spouse nicely even when he or she is being rude. Sometimes when things are not going the way we would want them to be, we tend to be rude to other people, even to our loved ones. This is also where you can exercise some kindness. Also, if it is your spouse who is having a bad day, then make sure to be there for him and comfort him.

You should also understand that you do not need to win an argument all the time. If you notice that a certain argument is not going somewhere desirable and that the subject is of little importance, then be kind enough to give way for your spouse.

You also need to realize that your spouse is not the enemy. He is on your side. He is there to help you and support you. Hence, it is only right and fair that you should treat each other kindly.

Kindness is a language that goes beyond the normal way people communicate. It is expressed not only through words but also through your actions. It is also noteworthy that every day and any time is a perfect moment to express some act of kindness to your loved one.

Train yourself to be kind even when it gets challenging to be kind. Kindness can get you a long way in marriage. In fact, if you are kind enough, there is a good chance that you will have a very good relationship with your spouse. Of course, you should also not forget that kindness should be accompanied by positive actions and not just empty words.

When the spouses are kind to each other, they easily make each other happy. Indeed, kindness is very effective in building a happy marriage. It is also not a secret that some people fall in love with a person once they recognize how truly kind he or she is. Kindness is much like love. It is placing your spouse before you and always considering what would be good for him or her. It is easy to be kind to one's spouse. After all, when you love a person, being kind to him or her would come naturally. And, just like love, kindness is free and has no limits.

16: Make Your Spouse Feel Important

By now it should already be clear to you that your spouse is one of the most important person in the world for you. It is only right that you let him or her know how important he or she is in your life. There are so many ways to do this. You can use words and tell him or her just how important he or she is to you and you can also express it through your actions. You can get him a gift, write him a letter, give him a massage, or simply treat him in a special way.

If you think that your spouse might not completely understand your kind gesture of love, then use words to make it very clear to him. The important thing is to make him know and feel that he or she is important in your life.

When a person is treated in a special way, it makes him feel important. It makes him feel loved. Hence, making your spouse feel important can do wonders for a relationship. Now, if it is your spouse who makes the move to make you feel just how important you are, make sure to express your appreciation. Although this is not related directly to communication, take note that improving the relationship can also improve the level of communication.

Another way to show your spouse just how important he is to you is by listening to him when he talks. A simple example of this is to stop whatever it is that you are doing when he talks to you. Of course, if you are the man, you should also do the same. These days, many couples do not talk properly. It is not uncommon to find couples who talk while the other person is watching a movie or reading a book. They fail to give 100% of their attention to each other. Yes, you can still engage in conversation and be responsive even while doing something else, but the point here is that you are not giving your spouse your full attention, and this does not make your spouse feel important. You should treat your spouse in a special way.

When you communicate with your spouse, it is always worth reminding yourself that you are talking to the most important person in your life. Unfortunately, many people fail to realize the value of their spouse and take every moment that they share together for granted. Make every moment count. Focus on your spouse and always treat him or her in a very special way.

Now, it is not uncommon for people to feel that they are probably no longer important to their spouse. This is true, especially when your spouse is so busy with work and other obligations that he or she has no time to enjoy life with you — and this is also wrong. Unfortunately, this has become common in many marriages these days. However, you should not let something like this to continue. If you feel like you are in this situation, then you should talk to your spouse about it. Another effective way is to be the one to show to your spouse just how important he is to you. You do not have to make things complicated or suffer in silence. Do not forget that your spouse is there for you. If you are not happy about something in your relationship, then face it together as a team.

It is noteworthy that making your spouse feel important takes positive actions on your part. Do not be content with just knowing that he is important to you, but you should communicate this message through your actions and in a way that will make him feel just how truly important he is in your life.

17: Give Time

Time is important in any relationship. Even if you are willing to work on your relationship, it would not be possible if you do not give it enough time. You need to have time so that you can talk and enjoy life with your spouse, etc. Although this may seem easy and simple, many couples have difficulty in doing it. Even if you have good intentions, things can change once you put in the time you need for work and other obligations that you "need" to do. The problem is that once you add all these things up, you may not have enough time left for your spouse. It is not uncommon to find people who get stuck up with lots of work and obligations. It is very easy to get busy in life that you will have no time to spend with your loved ones. Especially in the modern world, many things can add up to your stress levels and make you very busy.

It is important for you to give time to your relationship. If you cannot give time, then *make* time. There are no excuses for this. If you do not have the time, then there is no way you can make your relationship work. In this world, humans are governed by time. Therefore, you need to make sure to give time to be with your spouse. Take note that this is not just about giving time, but you also need to give sufficient time. A way to do this is by using time management and setting your priorities. In your set of priorities, place your spouse as the number one priority. This way it is already assured that you will have time for your spouse. Yes, you should consider your spouse to be more important than your work. If you still think that work should always come first, then that way of thinking is probably what is causing problems in your relationship.

This is not a license for you to be lazy and not do much work. Work is still a priority, but do not treat it as something that is more important than your spouse. Sometimes it can be unavoidable to get too busy with work. When this happens, just be sure to explain it to your spouse, and then make it a priority to make it up to him or her after some time. The important thing is to always make time to spend quality moments with your spouse. After all, what good is all the work if you do not even have time to go out on a date with the man/woman of your dreams? So, when you manage your time, your spouse should always be on top of the list. The reason here is that if you place your work as the main priority, then so many things can happen. In fact, work alone can consume your whole life if you really dedicate yourself to it. Be very careful how you spend your time. It is unfortunate that what many people fail to realize these days is that they spend so little time with their spouse. They get "too busy" with the demands of the modern world dealing with lots of stress and numerous obligations that simply have no end. If this ever happens to you, know that you have the power to make a difference. You do not have to answer all these demands. In fact, you can drop everything at once and just be with your spouse. If you are too busy to make time for your spouse, then you definitely have to make some changes in your life. Once again, make your spouse your number one priority.

It should also be noted that when you spend time with your spouse, be sure that you have all your attention on him. You should not be mentally absent. Hence, this is not the time for you to think about work or other things. So, for example, if you are going on a movie night, then use that time to relax with your spouse. Also, make your spouse laugh. Laughter has its own language and means that a person is having fun. Whatever time that you spend with your spouse, make sure to make it count.

18: Respect

Respect is very important in marriage. The moment that you start to lose respect for each other is also the moment when love begins to fade. Respect is important for both men and women. However, it is worth noting that men have a stronger need to be respected. Therefore, if you are the wife, make sure to give great respect to your husband. Of course, if you are the husband, you should also respect your wife as much as you can. After all, everyone desires to be respected.

It is not easy to respect someone who acts rudely. So, make sure that you are also worthy of respect. If you want to be respected, then you should also learn to respect your spouse, and do not do anything that would make your spouse lose his respect for you.

Be respectful at all times and avoid situations that can make you offend your spouse. Respect is a sensitive thing. If you lose it, then you can expect for your whole marriage to fail as well. Therefore, make sure that respect is present in your marriage. It is not enough that you know that you respect your spouse. You also need to show it. It is important for your spouse to feel that you respect him or her.

Respect is very important to men. Do not belittle your husband. Instead, speak highly of him. Make him feel that you believe in him. If you are the wife, then you need to trust your husband. Always be there to support him. Of course, this does not mean that you should still support him if he wants to do something that is not good. However, if your husband is in the pursuit of his dreams, especially if it is good for the family, then always let your husband know that you are there for him.

In any kind of relationship, respect always plays an important element. Always respect each other. Respect how your spouse thinks, feels, and talks. Be careful with your choice of words when talking with your spouse and avoid saying things that your spouse would find offending or insulting. Cultivate an atmosphere of trust and kindness. Make your spouse feel that you respect and love him or her completely.

A common mistake is to get too comfortable and forget about the respect that your spouse deserves. As a couple, it is only right that you get very comfortable with each other, but that does not mean that you will also forget about respecting each other. Respect is also a part of any loving relationship. Without respect, love would be hard to be felt.

19: Forgive

Forgiveness is also important in a relationship. You should never hold any grudge or resentment against your spouse; otherwise, you will not be able to hear him completely when he talks. It is natural for people to commit mistakes. From time to time, you will need to forgive your spouse to keep the relationship strong and full of love. Forgiveness is an act of love. As humans in a special relationship, mistakes are bound to happen. But, these mistakes are not completely bad. Mistakes can teach you the right way, the better way to a more meaningful marriage.

Another point: You should also forgive yourself. Without forgiveness, a person would tend to build walls, which is not good for building effective communication. You should understand that you forgive not only for the sake of your spouse but also for your own good. Holding on to anger or hatred for long is not good for you. After all, hating your spouse would not do your relationship any good.

Forgiveness may not always come easily. However, if you truly love your spouse, then there will always be room in your heart for forgiveness. Sometimes it may just take time before you can actually forgive your partner, but it is always possible. After all, when there is love, there is no offense that is so big that cannot be forgiven. But, of course, you should not abuse your spouse's kindness. Although forgiveness is always possible, a person has free will whether or not to exercise it. Therefore, just because you know that your spouse will forgive you does not mean that you can just do anything you want. You should still be sensitive to how your spouse would feel or think. Also, be grateful when you receive forgiveness. Keep in mind that your spouse is not obliged to extend to you any form of forgiveness. Hence, make sure that you learn from the experience, and do your best to improve yourself and be a better spouse.

In the course of your marriage, you can be sure to exercise some forgiveness from time to time. Sometimes you will have to forgive your spouse; while other times, you will be the one who will be asking for forgiveness. As mere humans, it is quite easy to commit mistakes, and this is normal. Just do your best to minimize it and always learn from every mistake. Granting forgiveness can be easy, especially when you consider just how much you really love your spouse. Forgive quickly and move on. Always love your spouse.

There is, however, a difference between forgiving and allowing your kindness to be abused by your spouse. Forgiving is good, but being abused is not. Hence, before you forgive your spouse, be sure that he or she knows exactly what he or she has done wrong. This is to ensure that he or she will learn from it and not do it again. Otherwise, there is a chance that your spouse will commit the very same mistake all over again. Of course, just because you have forgiven your spouse does not guarantee that he or she will no longer be able to commit the same mistake, but at least it would be minimized. After all, some bad habits are hard to break quickly.

The point here is to forgive and keep your relationship intact and make it even stronger.

20: Continuous Practice

It takes time and practice to build a strong bond. You may also find some of the techniques in the book easy to understand but hard to be put into practice. However, if you persist, then you will soon get used to these techniques. The key is to turn them into a habit.

Continuous practice is important. Do not be discouraged if you fail to apply the techniques in this book effectively in the first few times that you try them out. That is normal. The good news is that the more that you apply these techniques, the easier they will be. You will get good at them soon as long as you persist in your practice.

Building effective communication in marriage usually takes time and patience, especially if you come from a marriage where the level of communication is simply not good enough. However, keep in mind that it is possible for you to make things so much better. Of course, you will have to dedicate some time, effort, and put in some hard work. Still, your goal of improving your communication with your spouse is nonetheless doable and is well within your reach. It is just up to you whether you would take positive actions to achieve it.

You do not have to master all the techniques in this book at once. If you want, you can just choose one or two techniques to learn every day or every week, depending on your progress. The important thing is for you to start taking positive actions to improve your communication with your spouse, which can then improve your relationship altogether.

Do not rush. Building effective communication usually takes time. A common mistake is to simply desire to have a better communication with your spouse without actually taking the right positive actions to achieve it. You will have to make adjustments and even get yourself out of your comfort zone for this to work properly. If you find any of these techniques difficult to apply, do not be easily discouraged. The key is simply to persist in its application, and you will soon get used to it that it will be a second nature to you.

With all the 21 effective techniques in this book, you will surely be able to improve your communication with your spouse significantly. But, just like learning any other skill or technique, the ideas in this book need to be put into practice to truly learn them. Once again, continuous practice is the key. The more that you apply these techniques, the more that you will get used to them. If you stick to these techniques, you can soon improve the level of communication in your marriage. Once you have the knowledge, continuous practice is the next step.

There is no perfect time to start learning these techniques than now. Every time that you talk with your spouse is a chance for you to apply and master these techniques. As you may have already noticed, not all of the techniques directly involve having an active conversation with your spouse. There are techniques like making time and having quality time that focuses more on improving your relationship with your spouse. This is because by improving your relationship, you also get to improve your level of communication. After all, communication is not just about words or expressing yourself to each other; another thing that matters is how you feel about each other when you talk. To improve on this, you need to feel good about being with each other, which means that you will have to improve your connection/relationship.

The true meaning of continuous practice is turning these techniques into a habit so that they will be a part of who you are. After all, these techniques are not something that you do for a few weeks and then forget altogether once you have achieved your objective. Rather, they should become an integral part of your relationship. If you come to think of it, these techniques are actually basic and simple but have been forgotten by many. Through continuous practice, these things will be very natural to you. Also, there is no better way to encourage your spouse to also communicate effectively than using these techniques in a conversation. After all, these techniques are not one-sided but always consider what would be best for both spouses.

21: Love

It is love that binds the couple. In fact, the act of effective communication is a manifestation of love where you share your thoughts and emotions with each other. This is trust, knowing that there is no guarantee that your spouse will not break your heart in the future. In the same way, you also spend the time to listen to him/her not because you have read about effective communication, but because you love him so much that you want to spend your precious time hearing his voice and knowing his thoughts and feelings.

Even when all else fails, love can set things right. In fact, it is the love that you have for your spouse that will lead you to have a better bond and improved communication. Just the fact that you are reading this book right now only proves that you do love your spouse and that you are willing to take positive actions to make your relationship work. No matter how your relationship is doing right now, know that you can always make it last, as long as you truly love each other. Love is the power that binds your marriage, and it is also what connects you to each other. If there is only one thing that you should remember from this book, that is to love your spouse with all your heart. When you do, then all the techniques in this book will come naturally. If you just examine the techniques written in this book, you will recognize that they are all acts of love. This book only reminds you how to be a lover. In the modern time, it is quite easy to forget what it really means to love a person. Unfortunately, there are now so many preconceptions and ideas of how loving another should be that people have forgotten what it truly means to love.

If there is anything in the world that truly is valuable, then that is love. It is love that keeps you together and connects you to each other. Without love, no marriage will ever work regardless of how many communication techniques that you apply. But, if you have love, and if you give it enough time to express itself, then you will even find out other ways to improve your communication. The power of love is beyond any technique of communication. However, love cannot be forced. There is no way that you can have quality time with someone whom you do not even love. But, if you truly love your spouse, then you have a very good chance of making your marriage work.

Communication is also an act of love. This is another reason why you should improve your level of communication in your marriage. As you may already know, couples with poor communication are usually the ones who do not last long. When communication fails, love follows. But, the good news is that there is something that you can do about this. With your love for your spouse, you can turn a problematic relationship into a marriage that is full of love, kindness, and understanding. After all, love is a powerful force that can move mountains. Love is the key.

Conclusion

Thanks for making it through to the end of this book. I hope it was informative and the book was able to provide you with a lot of the tools you need to achieve your goals whatever they may be.

The next step is to apply everything that you have learned and have a happier marriage. The techniques in this book take practice for you to really learn them, and for you to be able to apply them effectively. Feel free to review these techniques and even modify them. Also, take note that communication is an art. As such, feel free to device your own technique that can help further improve your communication with your spouse. You may have to do some trial and error to identify the ones that work, as well as those that fail to make any positive impression.

I would also like to congratulate you because just the fact that you have reached this part of the book only goes to show that you truly value your relationship. In a relationship, especially in marriage, you really have to support each other every now and then. If communication is one of the things that your spouse is not very good at, then you should cover that part for him or her. The fact that you are reading this book means that you are doing your duty so well as the spouse. Remember not to give up on your marriage. By learning to communicate more effectively with your spouse, you will be able to experience a big improvement in your marriage. It is also an effective way to bring the fire of intimacy back into your marriage.

Marriage is sacred, and learning to communicate effectively with your spouse can both save a marriage from falling apart and can help you create a wonderful and happier marriage. If you truly love your spouse, then do not give up on him or her. Keep working on your communication techniques and keep trying. Do everything that you can to make your marriage work. It is not really difficult to improve the level of communication in marriage. By now you should already know the specific things that you need to do when you engage in a conversation with your spouse. You may not be able to notice the improvements right away, but you will definitely notice them over time. This book is not just a book about communication; it is a book about connection and love, and it teaches you to love your spouse with all your heart, mind, and soul.

Finally, if you found this book useful in any way, a review on Amazon is always appreciated!

77061537R00042

Made in the USA
Middletown, DE
17 June 2018